POWERFUL WORSHIP
—— IN THE ——
WAR ROOM

DANIEL B LANCASTER

Lightkeeper Books
Nashville, Tennessee

LIGHTKEEPER
BOOKS

LIGHTKEEPER
BOOKS

IN MEMORY OF
HOLLI SUZANNE LANCASTER

Precious Wife – Beloved Mother

TABLE OF CONTENTS

PREFACE

My prayer is this book will strengthen your walk with God. May you draw closer to Jesus every day and be filled with the Spirit. May you have a deep sense in your spirit that God loves you and will never let you go.

  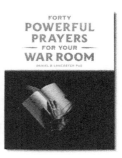

I have included several bonus gifts that I believe will be a blessing to you. The free *Powerful Prayers Bonus Pak* which includes three resources to help you pray powerful prayers:

- 100 Promises Audio Version
- 40 Faith-Building Quotes
- 40 Powerful Prayers.

All are suitable for framing. Download your free *Powerful Prayers Bonus Pak* at go.lightkeeperbooks.com/powerpak

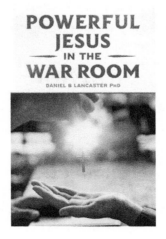

I've also included an excerpt from my book *Powerful Jesus in the War Room*. God has blessed many through this book and I wanted to give you a chance to "try before you buy." Order *Powerful Jesus in the War Room*, at go.lightkeeperbooks.com/e-pjw

If you like the book, please leave a review. Your feedback will help other believers find this book easier and encourage me in my calling to write practical, powerful books to encourage, equip, and empower Christians throughout the world.

Every Blessing,

Daniel B Lancaster
Nashville, Tennessee — August 2016

INTRODUCTION

*As many have learned and later taught, you don't
realize Jesus is all you need until Jesus is all you have.*

— TIM KELLER

Christianity sure seems complicated and cluttered today.

Everyone has an opinion about what you should or shouldn't do. There are books and tapes and sermons and church services and small groups, and the list goes on. Amid the swirl, I have often found myself in a spiritual desert and wondering how my life could be different.

Then I read what Paul said in 2 Corinthians 11:3: "I worry that you have left the simplicity of Christ." Maybe following Jesus should be simple after all.

That's what this book is all about. I want to show you how I and others have simplified our spiritual lives. A simple spiritual life is sustainable, nourishing, and will help you to flourish as a person.

My family spent 12 years on the mission field and learned many truths about ourselves and our walk with God. There's nothing like leaving your culture and being thrust into a completely new one to shake the chaff from the wheat! What we discovered disturbed us – many of the "truths" and "principles" we had heard in church all of our lives didn't work in another country. It led us to a crisis of belief.

That's when the simplicity of following Jesus became real to us. In this book, I want to share with you what we discovered. I believe it will set you free from the false expectations of cultural Christianity. You are going to be able to let go and let God take you places you could have never believed. Don't get me wrong, I still struggle in my walk with Jesus. But walking with Him in a simpler way has allowed me to find true north much easier and to move towards becoming a healthier person.

I'm going to share with you some of the same lessons we learned and taught to over 5,000 national believers in Southeast Asia. God worked in our friends to start over 1,200 discipleship groups and 200 churches. More than that, our family grew in Christ together amid incredibly difficult times.

I believe as you read and apply the simple spiritual habits we will talk about in this book, you are going to experience new freedom in your life. Not some emotional one-and-done, but continual rivers of living water. You will experience the joy of walking in simplicity with Jesus. As you de-clutter your life and live more simply, you will have more time for the relationships in life that really matter.

When God called our family of six to move overseas as missionaries, our children were eleven, nine, seven, and four years old at the time. That move was, as I'm sure you understand, a giant leap of faith.

We sold our house and two cars and gave most of our other belongings away. The country we moved to did not allow crates to be sent from the United States. It was considered one of the top five worst military dictatorships in the world.

As a result, our family packed everything into nineteen suitcases, boarded a plane, and left for Southeast Asia to start a new life. Although we left a few household memories in storage back in America, those nineteen suitcases represented a return to a simpler life.

Life was not easy. Soldiers with machine guns stood guard at every major intersection in the capital city. Insurgents detonated a bomb in a store my wife had left only thirty minutes earlier, killing seventeen of the clerks and managers. We removed three cobras from the front flower bed where our kids normally played. Secret police followed us everywhere and would question the national friends we spent time with after we had left their homes.

But many years later, our whole family will tell you it is the best move we ever made. Living overseas simplified our lives, drew us closer as a family, and strengthened our faith.

I can't think of a better time to simplify your life and find true happiness than right now, can you? The following pages will give you practical ways to simplify your spiritual life, make the changes into habits, and watch God transform your life.

If your spiritual life is cluttered and feels like a desert, I know that reading this will help you because it has helped me and others just like you. Let's start by looking at the foundation of a simple spiritual life – loving God.

1

LOVING GOD

Living simply makes loving simple.

— BELL HOOKS

Everyone wants to be loved and to love others. The problem is we have hurts, habits, and hang-ups that keep us from love. We end up feeling lonely, disconnected, and miserable.

In this chapter, I want to show you how to break the chains that are holding you back. We're going to look at the Great Commandment and see how God will heal you as you obey Him.

God loves you and wants you to experience His love. In fact, God is the source of love, so it is important you receive love from Him, so you can give love to the people in your life. Love problems are always God problems.

I come from a broken home and have found loving God, myself, and others difficult at times — that is until I started obeying the Great Commandment in practical ways. My wife and I taught our kids to do the same, and they continue to follow Jesus and share the love of God to this day. I also have seen what you will learn in this chapter transform thousands of people's lives.

When you finish reading this chapter, you will have learned a practical way to experience the love of God. You will have simple truths that you can fall back to when you are hurting, facing a crisis, or feeling betrayed by a friend. No matter where you find yourself in life, you will have a simple and powerful way to connect with God.

I remember a Bible training event that took place while we were missionaries in Southeast Asia. It was in a remote area that took three hours to reach by air, followed by a ten-hour bus trip to the foot of a mountain. Finally, we took a two-hour motorcycle ride to the village church that was hosting the training.

A few days before the start of the Bible training, I called the pastor and told him I would not be able to come. I had the flu with a high temperature, ached all over my body, and felt weak. We needed to postpone the training. His reply surprised me.

He said, "We can't postpone the training."

Usually, Asian pastors are gracious and don't address missionaries in a direct way like this. I knew for him to say "we can't" went against his culture and upbringing.\

I said, "You don't understand. I have the flu and a high temperature. My whole body is aching, and I feel weak."

He said, "I am sorry for that, brother. We will pray that God heals you, but we cannot postpone the training. Believers have been walking through the jungle for a week to attend the training, and I have no way to tell them we have canceled it. You must come."

I prayed about whether I should go or not again and ended up going to the training. We had twelve participants, and they started eleven churches in the following months. God gave me the strength to persevere.

During our time as foreign missionaries, we normally only saw local believers once. We traveled around the country and Southeast Asia, rarely returning to the same place a second time.

I realized this meant we likely only had one chance with each person. God pricked my heart, asking, "If you could train believers how to obey only one command of Jesus, which one would you choose?" One command? Teach and practice just ONE spiritual habit that would result in believers obeying all the rest of Jesus's commands?

Eventually, we decided the "one command" to teach was the Great Commandment. If a person simply obeyed the Great Commandment to love God with all their heart, soul, mind, and strength, they would flourish as a Christ-follower.

In this chapter, I will show you what we learned and taught our children and others. I'm excited because you are going to be blessed as you apply the Great Commandment in your life. God is going to bring healing, strength, confidence, and joy for you like He has many others.

So, let's look at the Great Commandment, and at how you can let God simplify your spiritual life.

THE GREAT COMMANDMENT

The first step in simplifying your spiritual life and strengthening your faith is experiencing the love of God.

Love is the cornerstone of real happiness and authentic spirituality. The more you receive and give love, the deeper you will grow spiritually. My prayer is that you will find greater love in your life.

Unfortunately, true love is hard to come by for most people. And that leads us to do desperate things while trying to find love, even when we know those choices will hurt us. Satan uses this against us all the time. He tempts us to sin and laughs in glee when we do, knowing we feel even more unlovable and unloved by God. I don't have to tell you it can be a vicious cycle and hard to overcome.

Deep down we know that love is the answer to our problem, but we often feel helpless or unable to love or be loved. We try hard but fail. I used to think I had to love through my own effort. Thankfully, God has provided another way. The Bible says in I John 4:7-8:

> *Dear friends, let us love one another, because love is from God, and everyone who loves has been born of God and knows God. The one who does not love does not know God, because God is love. (HCSB)*

The good news is that love comes from God first. When we love God or another person, we are merely taking the love we have already received from God and giving it away.

We receive love from God and give love back to Him. We receive love from God and give it to others. Simple. Powerful. This is how God created love to work.

When we find it hard to love God or people, typically we aren't receiving or accepting enough of the love of God in our life. The problem isn't that we can't give love, but that we haven't received enough love to be able to give love away. We will return to this spiritual principle many times in this book.

It is important to keep the "we receive love to give love" principle in mind when you read the Great Commandment in Mark 12:38-41:

> *One of the teachers of the law came and heard them debating. Noticing that Jesus had given them a good answer, he asked Him, "Of all the commandments, which is the most important?" "The most important one," answered Jesus, "is this: 'Hear, O Israel, the Lord our God, the Lord is one. Love the Lord your God with all your heart and with all your soul and with all your mind and with all your strength.' The second is this: 'Love your neighbor as yourself.' There is no commandment greater than these."*

Jesus shares the most important command that anyone can obey: love God with everything you are and do. Considering the Pharisees of the time taught that "true believers" had to obey 633 different commands, Jesus simplified everything quite a bit.

Let's look at how we can obey the command to love God with all our heart, soul, mind, and strength. Obeying the Great Commandment is the key to finding true love.

WITH YOUR HEART

Loving God with all your heart means that you love Him with that part of you that feels deeply, that hopes and cares, and that is burdened when your life isn't right.

The hand motion for loving God with all your heart is pictured below. Put both of your hands on your heart.

The first part of the Great Commandment is loving God with all your heart.

Your heart can be broken, hurting, and closed – or – your heart can be open, full, and overflowing. God sent His Son, so your heart could be free and flowing like a river of living water. That is God's will for you.

I can remember times in my life when my heart was light, and I felt like I was walking on clouds. I felt a great love for everyone and felt great joy. Those times make the best memories a person can have while living in this broken world. You can probably remember times like those in your life, too.

Sadly, though, troubles weighed my heart down much of the time and made it hard to love God. I hope you haven't experienced that, but I know that most people have.

Satan shackles our heart in so many ways. Maybe when you were growing up, it wasn't OK to share how you really felt, and this locked your heart down. Or maybe you found yourself in situations where you had to "perform" for others and didn't feel like you could be the real you, so your heart developed walls to protect yourself. I've listed just a few examples of the shackles that can make it hard to love God with all our heart.

One of the ways people deal with their heart pain is by trying to fill their lives with accomplishments or material possessions to prove they are valuable. Surely, they think "if I do valuable work or have wealth, I am valuable myself." What ends up happening, however, is hurting people who are over-committed at work and overwhelmed with credit card debt. Their lives have become complicated and confusing, and they feel trapped.

So, you hear this command and think "I would like to love God with all my heart, but I don't think I can. I have too much hurt holding me back." There is a way to simplify your life, and it starts with loving God with all your heart. And it is easier than you might think.

God is love, and His heart's desire is that you experience His love. True love always brings healing. The more time you spend with God and let Him love you, the more you will be healed and be able to return His love.

Picture yourself walking in a forest filled with tall trees and beautiful flowers. The forest is quiet except for the sweet sound of birds calling. As you walk along the path, you see a mountain spring and decide to sit down and enjoy the relaxing sound of the water running across the rocks.

You feel your heart become strangely warm as Jesus sits down beside you. Both of you are quiet for several minutes, just enjoying each other's company and watching the mountain spring.

Then Jesus turns and says, "Tell me what is on your heart."

At first, you share just a little because your experience with other people has been that they don't really want to hear everything. So, you aren't sure if Jesus wants to hear about the feelings you want to share. You think that maybe He is just saying that.

During your conversation, however, He says "tell me more" several times, and you finally understand that He truly wants to know you, the real you. He loves you and wants to hear about everything on your heart.

You feel the fears begin to melt away; the perfectionism begins to loosen its hold; and the desire for anything but sharing time with Jesus fades. You see clearly how empty performing to prove yourself is. You see how the things you own have really been owning you.

Rivers of living water flow from your heart. Rivers of love flow between you and Jesus.

As you get up to walk home, Jesus smiles and gives you a hug.

"Let My heart heal your heart," He says.

You go home with a heart that wants to love God and love others. Loving is simpler than you thought.

Anytime you feel your heart is hard and pulling away from God, it is a sign that you have allowed your heart to become cluttered. Let perfectionism and wanting more possessions fall to the side and accept a God-healed heart.

Jesus doesn't expect you to come to Him perfectly; He just wants to spend time with you because He loves you. He knows you have tried to fill the hole in your heart with glitter and gold. But He doesn't condemn. Jesus wants you to simplify your life, so you will have more time with Him and the people you love.

Let me encourage you to go today to the stream that never runs dry and find that wonderful living water for your parched heart. God will help you and heal you as you love Him with all your heart.

WITH YOUR SOUL

The next part of the Great Commandment is to love God with all your soul. Bible scholars debate what the soul is and its location in the human body. In fact, scholars have many differing opinions. With so much disagreement, how can we decide how to love God with all our soul?

For me, I look at how Jesus lived and what He said about the soul. Jesus prayed in the Garden of Gethsemane the night before He was crucified, saying "My soul is greatly distressed unto death" (Matthew 26:38). I don't know about you, but when I am praying fervently, I feel something in my stomach. For that reason, this is the hand motion we use to depict loving God with all your soul:

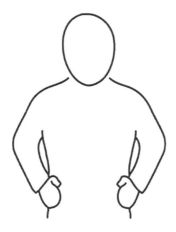

Now, I'm not saying some people have bigger souls than other folks. Nor am I saying if you are thin you have a small soul. What I am saying is one of the places the soul expresses itself is in your stomach. It is the place you feel when you are praying like you have never prayed before. Some examples of these times are after you learn of a dear friend's auto accident or perhaps find out a family member has a major illness.

Some people sell their soul to the devil, while other people are called "kind souls". You can have an old soul, a tired soul, or be a kindred soul. You can bare your soul or pour out your soul, and confession is good for the soul. Maybe you are the life and soul of the party or people call you a soul brother.

I think our soul is that part of us that gives us willpower and the ability to keep going in difficult times. The soul helps us keep commitments our minds have decided are important. That is why Jesus also prayed in the Garden of Gethsemane, "Not my will, but Thine" (Matthew 26:39). Your soul has a deep sense of the mission God sent you into this world to fulfill.

When our family learned that my wife had ovarian cancer, I felt like all the wind had been taken out of my sails. I lost all motivation and energy. My soul grieved, and everything turned gray and gloomy. Have you experienced something life-shattering like that before? If you have, I pray that God will somehow help you see the sunshine again.

Sadly, it is easy for our broken world to damage your soul. You may have given up on your life. You may have said, "Nothing I do matters any way. Everything always turns out wrong." You may have found yourself thinking the world would be a better place if you weren't alive. Like George Bailey in the movie It's a Wonderful Life, you may find yourself saying, "I want to live again. I want to live again."

We as humans try several coping strategies when our soul is damaged. Some people decide they must take life by the reins - become the master of their soul – and try to control everything. Others want to escape life and the suffering in their soul, so they disconnect with drugs, or alcohol, or pornography, or anything that helps them forget the pain.

The problem is... none of this works. Controlling things and people may work for a while, but soon the soul begins to cry out for something more. Trying to escape life ends in bondage. Many people find themselves empty after trying these coping strategies and still searching. If we are honest, we are all in that place more than we like to admit.

So how do you love God with all your soul when it is broken?The answer is spending time with the lover of your soul –God Himself. He created each of us with a place inside us bigger than the universe. The feelings I have been talking about are homesickness for God.

A parched soul is the sign of someone who has not drank from the river of living water lately. Not spending time with the One who bore your burdens on the cross creates a heavy soul. Your soul is the map God has placed in you and your sense of purpose. Spending time with the Great Mapmaker is the key to a healthy, vibrant soul.

Imagine a family that is crazy busy. Dad works hard and gets promotions. Mom is president of the local school's parent association and heavily involved in her children's lives. The children play soccer, basketball, and baseball. They also take ballet and gymnastics. One of mom's full-time jobs is just running them from place to place. But the family feels empty, so they watch TV whenever they can, go to the movies, go to amusement parks, and organize outings to somehow feel like a "real family". They rush to church and home and school and every other place. Every day is busy, then they go to sleep, and then they repeat everything the next day.

One Saturday morning, mom and dad decide to get some coffee at Starbucks. They are sipping their lattes when Jesus approaches them and asks if He can sit down with them. Surprised, they say yes.

Sitting down, Jesus says, "What would it gain a man and woman if they did everything American culture says you have to do to be good parents and lost their soul? You are so overwhelmed with your schedule that you don't see or hear beauty anymore."

"We were just talking about that. We don't want that life any longer," the man answers.

With tears, the wife says, "But we don't know how to stop."

Jesus looks at them both and smiles. "I will help you. Let me show you how to live a simple life in Me. I promise your kids will be richer for it, and both of you will enjoy a marriage you never thought possible. Let me give you rest. Spend time with me, and I will show you how to love God with all of your soul."

I believe Jesus wants to give you rest, my friend. My family had the benefit of living 12 years overseas and not feeling the pull of the American culture machine. We could live simply then and continue to do so since coming back to America. Doing so allowed us to live unhurriedly and always ready for deep talks and special friendships. I find myself often praying that we will not fall into the trap of thinking that what we do defines our lives. A simple life remembers living is about who we are, not what we do.

So, let me encourage you to love God with all your soul. Let go and let God move in your life. Don't fall for the empty promises of the ways this world tries to heal the soul. Let the One who knows every part of you give you purpose and peace, rest and refreshing, healing and hope.

WITH YOUR MIND

After the heart and soul, Jesus says to love God with all your mind. Most of us understand the mind more than we do the heart and soul. We think with our mind, study with our mind, memorize with our mind, read with our mind, and renew our mind if we are followers of Jesus.

Put your right hand and left hand on both sides of your head for the "with your mind" hand motion. This hand motions reminds us to love God with all our mind.

Our mind stores our beliefs about ourselves as pictures – our self-image. People with a good self-image see their strengths and weaknesses. People with a poor self-image usually see only their weaknesses. The mind is a battlefield with Satan, and he tries everything he can to trick and deceive believers. He is the father of lies and lies take root in the mind.

Satan will do anything to stop a believer from loving God with all their mind. I know this from personal experience. My parents divorced when I was a teenager, and Satan used this to convince me that I wasn't loved and that it was my fault. Having stayed with my father, I felt abandoned by him after my first semester at college. I felt the pain of a broken family intensely and struggled with depression for many years.

If you feel that way now, I want you to know that I understand how hard it can be to love God with all your mind. This is especially true if events in your life have left you traumatized. Convincing your mind to trust people again can be hard.

God created us with minds full of creativity, exploration, analysis, and emotional intelligence. He created us with the capacity to be transformed in His presence. The Lover of Your Soul loves to see you deepen your friendship with Him and others. To some, He gave the mind to play instruments; to others, He gave writing, the ability to solve difficult math problems, or a quick wit to tell jokes that make everyone laugh.

Tragically, the abilities of our minds turned against us after sin entered the world. Now, we can't stop thinking, and so we have panic attacks. Now, we can't stop our thoughts, and we struggle with worry. Now, we have impure pictures in our mind and are overcome with lust. Now, we copy the world and Satan's schemes instead of being transformed by renewing our mind. Now, Satan has us convinced that we can trust no one and will never be safe. Everything is changing around us, and we feel insecure.

You can love God with all your mind, though. You can let God's promises and truth renew your mind. You can overcome any addiction that started in your mind by cutting it down at the root. You can learn to be kind to yourself and see yourself the way God sees you – loved and cherished. You have the mind of Christ and can be creative, loving, and wise.

God's thoughts are so much higher than ours, and He will change your mind if you come to Him. He promises to restore and forgive when we repent. God has sent you His Holy Spirit to guide you into truth – into everything that is right and good and strong. God made up His mind a long time ago that He was going to save you, restore you, and love you forever. I don't think anything in the Universe can keep Him from doing this, do you? He is so much bigger than the mountains you have built in your mind. So much bigger, friend.

Imagine a delightful garden with fountains, footpaths, towering trees, and beautiful flowers. Imagine benches to sit on in the shade and squirrels playing hide-and-go-seek.

Then, imagine angels softly singing and playing instruments that make the most beautiful music imaginable. Peace. Faith. Hope. Love. Joy.

But then see an evil, sinister force enter the garden and begin to sow weeds. Watch the evil one chop down trees and set fire to the wooden gazebos. He cuts down the flowers, upturns the rocks on the path, and hangs pictures of suffering and sorrow throughout the garden.

All the while, he snickers and sings a song that leaves every part of you empty, hopeless, and lonely. He tears and shreds and burns until the garden looks desolate – nothing like what it was in the beginning. Anytime good tries to grow, the evil one swoops down and destroys it. Desolation. Loneliness. Ugliness. Wickedness. Despair.

But one day, a Man comes into the garden and begins to till the soil again. The garden has yearned for this Man for a long time and has called to Him. Everything has been destroyed for as far as the eye can see. Everything except the place the Man works.

Gently, reverently, lovingly, the Man restores the garden. He fixes the broken benches and gazebo. He plants new trees and flowers. He even takes the burned parts of the garden and uses them to bring new life. Little by little, the garden comes alive under the careful skill of the Man. It takes time, but the result is more beautiful than the garden was in the beginning.

Our minds are that garden. Satan had cast a shadow over our minds and led us away into darkness. We were alienated from God in our minds and full of prejudice, condemnation, bitterness, and devotion to God's enemy. We ourselves had become enemies of God. But, God in His great love sent His Son, who saved us. Now He is working on our mind to bring back everything that is right. Loving God with all your mind brings the beauty back to your garden.

I don't know what is holding you back today from loving God with all your mind. In our world, it could be a thousand different things. But I want you to stop and think about what I have shared in this section. Be honest with yourself. All of us have footholds that allow Satan to capture our thinking if we leave them unguarded. Are you free, or are you trapped?

In the next chapter, I'm going to share how you can develop simple spiritual habits that free your mind from Satan's evil schemes, but first let's talk about loving God with all your strength.

WITH YOUR STRENGTH

The last part of the Great Commandment is loving God with all your strength. You love God with your strength in your work, hobbies, talents, social connections, and how you spend your time. Everything you do is a sacrifice of praise and a gift of love to Him.

The hand motion for "loving God with all your strength" is above. Picture a weight lifter flexing their muscles to show how strong he or she is, and you'll understand the hand motion.

Your strength is the ability to keep going when circumstances are rough. The struggles we have today give us strength for tomorrow. It's in the hard battles of life that we realize God is our source of strength. In times of sickness, financial difficulties, or friendship problems, we learn to love God and trust in His love for us.

Many years ago, I was diagnosed with a disease called Ankylosing Spondylitis – rheumatoid arthritis of the hip joints, spine, and rib cage. I felt like all the strength in my body had drained away and been replaced by constant pain. You can probably understand the questions and cries for mercy that became a part of my life. I often thought, Why God? All I want to do is serve you, God, but this pain makes it so difficult.

Although I wouldn't wish what I went through on anyone, I can tell you I learned so much about receiving and giving the love of God during my suffering. God has healed my body now, and I am grateful, but I wouldn't trade the lessons I learned in those years of anguish for anything.

Some find it hard to love God with all their strength because of a hurtful past. Maybe you were teased a lot as a child and developed a thick outer layer to protect yourself. You come across as strong, but you really aren't, and you fear people will discover your secret.

Or maybe you were betrayed by someone you loved and have decided you have to be strong, so you will never be hurt again. You would rather people fear you than take a chance on feeling fear yourself.

Those ways of coping are not the strength Jesus is talking about in the Great Commandment. Jesus is talking about strength that comes from knowing you are loved by God. When you know that love, your greatest passion is to give everything – all your strength – back in loving Him. You realize God has rescued you, and you don't have to be the rescuer any longer. When you embrace God's strength, it is made perfect in your weakness.

God knows the battles you have been fighting inside that no one else sees. He is a Rock that will never leave you. He has sent His Holy Spirit to comfort you and give you the power to keep going. He is the Great Shepherd and loves to protect and provide everything you need. You don't need to fear being harmed or controlled by others any longer. Begin giving your strength to trusting in God and stop trying to force or control your life.

God created our bodies in a special way. Repeatedly doing something creates a habit. Habits help us to do tasks without thinking about them. That is good, of course, when it is a good habit. Addictions are bad practices that have become habits in our lives and are destroying us.

What all of us need to do is to let our good habits become so much a part of us that we don't think about doing the good any longer. We just do it. We need to form simple spiritual habits. Each of us has a choice when bad things happen – we can either become bitter or better. Simple spiritual habits help us become better. Loving God with all our strength is all about developing those kinds of simple spiritual habits in our lives.

I started this chapter by talking about the hurts, hang-ups, and habits we have in our lives that steal love. We have a love problem today, and it is causing people to seek solutions in desperation – most of which leave them far worse off than before. Never have people had more money, and never have we felt less loved. What can we do?

The answer is to obey the Great Commandment by receiving love from God and giving it back to Him. We love Him with our heart, soul, mind, and strength. I have shared what I and others have learned practically in each of those areas. It's a start, and I look forward to hearing from you about the truths God shows you about loving Him.

When we love God, it changes us for the better from the inside out. We become more like Him. He mends our heart, strengthens our soul, sharpens our mind, and gives us a passion to do great things for His kingdom. We start on a journey that is life-giving and deeply satisfying. We may not have many material possessions, but we have the Pearl of Great Price, and it is enough.

Let me share a story about someone who found true riches....

One afternoon, I received a phone call from the wife of an elderly man who was on his deathbed (let's call him Mark). She asked if I could go and visit him. She wasn't sure about his soul and wanted me to help him prepare for the afterlife. So, I drove several miles down a country road until I came to Mark's white-board house.

Mark's wife invited me into the house and went to the kitchen to fix some coffee for both of us. He was sitting in an easy chair in his living room, clearly in pain. His wife's eyes filled with tears when she brought us the coffee and then quietly excused herself.

Mark and I talked for a while about his life – his family, where he had worked, what his hobbies had been.

After a while, I asked Mark for his thoughts on the afterlife. He assured me he was ready and looked forward to going to a place with no more suffering and sorrow. He looked forward to seeing Jesus face-to-face. He had led a full life and felt like it was time to go home.

Thankful to hear he had peace about his future, I asked him,

"Mark, you are an old man, and I am a young man. If there was only one piece of advice you could give me, what would it be?"

He thought about my question for several minutes and smiled saying,

"Dan don't worry about money. The money will always take care of itself. Worry instead about whether you have good friends or not. A good friend is priceless."

He went on to give me several examples of when God had provided financially in his life and told me humorous stories about his good friends.

Two weeks later, I officiated at Mark's funeral and could comfort his family with the assurance he had been ready for heaven.

Mark's advice has been one of a few guiding principles for my life since. Relationships are what matter, and simplifying your life gives you more time with people and with God. If having friends is important, imagine how important being a friend of God is for a healthy life.

In the end, love is all that really matters. Obeying the Great Commandment is the surest sign that you understand that truth.

We have covered the four parts of our lives that Jesus commands us to love God with passionately. It might seem a tall order to you. For many years, I knew about the Great Commandment but had no concrete way to obey it. I knew it was important but didn't know how to apply it in my life. In the next chapter, I'll show you how that all changed for me, and I believe it will change for you too.

2

POWERFUL WORSHIP

Do few things but do them well, simple joys are holy.
— ST. FRANCIS OF ASSISI

If you're like me, you have heard countless sermons through the years and been told what you should and should not do. Obeying the Great Commandment is usually at the top of the "you should do this" list. But the problem is that, too often, no one shows us how to obey. I'm not criticizing preachers (I am one after all) but simply pointing out a weakness in the way we do church.

In this chapter, I want to show you a way to obey the Great Commandment that has transformed my life, my family's lives, and the lives of thousands of people we have trained. It's called Powerful Worship.

We discovered Powerful Worship by accident while we were on the mission field. During the time we were in Myanmar, it was illegal for Christians to meet in groups larger than five people. We had become convinced that teaching people to obey the Great Commandment was our main mission. But we had to figure out how to do it in a way that people wouldn't be breaking the law.

We wanted to teach believers a way to strengthen their spiritual life that was simple and easy to pass on to others, even if someone only had a third-grade education. We wanted them to be doers of the word and not hearers only. We didn't want to "educate" them beyond what they could obey.

I am going to show you what we practice and taught others in this chapter – how to set up "simple spiritual habits" in your life. Let me warn you from the start – what you are going to learn is very simple. But that is the power of Powerful Worship – anyone can do it, and the more they do, the more love for God will fill their lives.

In fact, Powerful Worship is so simple, we thought at first that only people with little education would embrace what we taught. Were we ever wrong.

A missionary friend of mine taught a group of doctors and lawyers in the Philippines how to celebrate Powerful Worship with their friends. My friend asked them to practice Powerful Worship together several times. He told me later about how he had been afraid of teaching doctors and lawyers something so simple. He was afraid they might be offended and think the training was too simple.

After the training, several of the doctors and lawyers in the room approached my friend. They told him, "Thank you for teaching us something that we can teach others! We are excited about this and look forward to starting Powerful Worship groups throughout the Philippines."

I am thankful to report the group of lawyers and doctors did start 68 new Powerful Worship groups over the next six months, and several of them became house churches.

My friend was celebrating God's goodness and reported this had happened while he was on furlough.

I could share so many similar stories with you and want you to know that I'm excited about what you are going to learn in this chapter. Sharing Powerful Worship with your friends is going to change you and them. It is going to strengthen and simplify your Christian life. You are going to discover a tool that will make your church stronger and your prayer group more powerful in spiritual warfare.

So, let's not waste any time. Let me take you through the instructions I have given people all over the world. We lost count a long time ago of how many Powerful Worship groups there are on every continent. I am believing you will start one too – you will taste and see the Lord is good as you worship Him with the simplicity of Christ.

WORSHIP

The first part of Powerful Worship is praising God. I have found that one of the easiest ways to show God how much I love Him (to love Him with all my heart) is through worship songs. As I begin to thank and praise Him, my heart opens, and love pours out. We love God with all our heart, so we worship him.

Here is the hand motion I use to remember this part of Powerful Worship. Place your hands over your heart, and then raise them in worship.

Before you start Powerful Worship with your group, agree on one person who will lead the worship time. They should choose songs that everyone knows and enjoys singing. They can lead the group with a guitar or keyboard, use a CD, or sing with no instruments. The goal is for everyone to love God with all their heart. Worshiping God helps us to do that easily.Each time your Powerful Worship group meets, a different person should lead the worship time. Take turns each time you meet until everyone has had an opportunity to lead, then continue to change it up every time you meet. This will keep the worship fresh and new each time. It will also allow everyone to practice leading worship in a small group and gain confidence. Look in the Frequently Asked Questions section to see how you can adapt the worship time if children or youth are leading.

PRAYER

After the first person has led worship, practice loving God with all your soul by praying together. Another person in the group should lead this part of Powerful Worship (not the person who led the worship time).

The "prayer" person asks each person for prayer requests and writes them down. The "prayer" person should also share any requests they have. Then, they pray fervently for each group member. They commit to interceding for the group for each request until the next meeting. Group members should also feel free to call or contact the "prayer" person between meetings to update or add to their prayer requests.

Use this hand motion to remind everyone about the goal of this part of Powerful Worship. We love God with all our soul, so we pray. Place your hands on your side, and then raise them in the classic "praying hands" position.

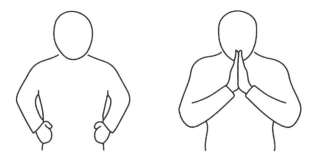

A benefit of meeting in Powerful Worship with two to four people is each person has plenty of time to share their prayer needs and have them prayed for by the group. Introverts and extroverts both share in a group this size and feel comfortable. This size group also helps prevent more task-oriented people from thinking the group is wasting time by recording dozens of prayer requests. More relationship-oriented people will enjoy the unity a small group provides. In either case, storm the gates of Hell in spiritual warfare together!

STUDY

A practical way to love God with all your mind is to study the Bible with your Powerful Worship group. The group should choose another person (not the worship person or the "prayer" person) to lead the study time. Group members should rotate through leading the different parts of Powerful Worship regularly.

Here is the hand motion to help remind us of the purpose of the study time in Powerful Worship. We love God with all our mind, so we study His word to become more like Him.

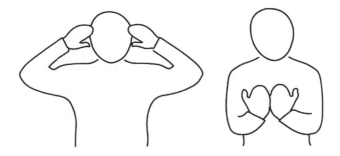

Yet another gentle warning. I recommend that you use bible stories for the study time, especially stories in the gospels about Jesus. This isn't the place for a Beth Moore bible study (although they are good)! In my experience, most believers in America know far more about the Bible than they obey. Better to know a little and obey it, than to know a lot and obey a little. For too long, we have centered our teaching on following principles rather than a person. When you follow principles, you are in charge. When you follow a person, they are.

After the "study" person has told the bible story, they should ask the group three questions:

1. What does this story teach us about God?
2. What does this story teach us about people?
3. How does this story help us follow Jesus?

The "study" person asks each question above, and the group answers. Take your time at this point and let everyone in the Powerful Worship group share something on each question. A group member might say, "I don't know," and that is fine.

We just want to make sure everyone feels valued and listened to during the discussion.

PRACTICE

Now it is time for the practice part of Powerful Worship – the most important part, in our opinion. So far, your group has worshiped, prayed, and studied the Bible. Most small group bible studies or Sunday School classes do the same. The reason Powerful Worship is different (and more fruitful) than what you usually experience in a small group time is the practice section. A fourth person (who has not led worship, prayed, or shared the bible story) should lead the practice time.The hand motions for the practice time are below. We want to love God with all our strength, so we practice what we have learned to share it with our friends and family. Put your arms out like you are lifting weights or flexing your biceps. Then, act as if you are casting seeds with your right hand.

Typically, we go back over what we learned in the "study part" of Powerful Worship in the practice part. Most people are more familiar with singing and praying than they are leading a small group in a bible study, so practice is important. We also know the Word of God is what changes people when they believe in faith. Repeating the bible story builds faith as we hear the Word of God again.

So, the practice person tells the same bible story the study person did. We encourage them to make telling the story dramatic and interesting. Picture yourself with your friends around a campfire telling stories at midnight, and you'll get the idea. After the practice person tells the same story, they ask the same three questions as before. Each person discusses each question just like before, too. Repeating the story gives everyone the opportunity to clear up misunderstandings from the first time through the story. It also gives the chance for group members to share any insights they may have received during the second telling.

After training more than 5,000 people in Powerful Worship, I have heard the same comment countless times. Students share their joy at how God uses the practice time to give them deeper insight into His word. They talk about a deeper sense of faith and a gained confidence to share the story. Sharing and discussing the story a second time also allows more mature believers in the group gently to correct unbiblical ideas that have been presented.

Powerful Worship ends with the group singing another song together (led by the worship person) or saying the Lord's Prayer together (led by the prayer person). Sometimes groups do both.

▼ ▼ ▼ ▼ ▼

Fear less, hope more, eat less, chew more, whine less, breathe more, talk less, say more, love more, and all good things will be yours.

– SWEDISH PROVERB

I struggled many years with how to obey the Great Commandment. Christians talked about how important it was but never gave me practical direction on how to obey.

Then, God showed our family and friends Powerful Worship. Through worship, prayer, bible study, and practicing what we had learned, we could obey the Great Commandment. We also found we could teach any believer Powerful Worship, and they could use it at home with their families, or with their small group, or at church to strengthen the Body of Christ.Now, many years later, the fruit of practicing Powerful Worship is everywhere. My children know how to minister to a small group and grow their faith. Many nationals we trained have used Powerful Worship to start new churches. Believers tell me repeatedly the joy they have found through obeying the Great Commandment. Not obedience in a legalistic way, but a way that deepens their friendship with God and people.

I remember a Follow Jesus training session we held in Myanmar. During the training, participants practiced Powerful Worship seven times. At the end of our time together, I asked if they had any questions.

The trainees asked me, "Dr. Dan, can we do Powerful Worship in our homes?"

I said, "Yes. Powerful Worship is great at home."

Then, they asked me, "Dr. Dan, can we do Powerful Worship in a restaurant?"

I said, "Yes. I know people who have practiced Powerful Worship in a restaurant after hours, and it led to a church."

They asked me, "Dr. Dan, can we do Powerful Worship under a mango tree?"

I said, "Absolutely. You can have Powerful Worship anywhere."

Then, the students asked me, "Dr. Dan, can we practice Powerful Worship at the Buddhist temple?"

A large, famous Buddhist temple looked out over the city from a mountaintop. You could see the temple from anywhere in the city, and its lights burned day and night.

I stopped. Several sticky problems with their question raced through my mind. I thought a minute, and then I said,

"You can have Powerful Worship anywhere God leads you."

After our team left the city, the students gathered for prayer. As they prayed, they sensed God saying to have Powerful Worship in the Buddhist temple. So, four of them went up the mountain on a Sunday night to worship the living God in the famous Buddhist temple.

One of the students started the Powerful Worship time by leading the group in worship songs to Jesus. In a Buddhist temple, many people mill around and socialize. As the Powerful Worship group began to love God with all their heart by worshiping, some Buddhists interrupted them.

"What are you doing?" they asked.

"We are worship the Living God with all of our heart like He has commanded," my friends replied.

"We like those songs," replied the Buddhists. "We have never heard them before, and they feel good to us."

After the worship time, the second trainee asked his friends for prayer requests. By this time, more Buddhists had joined the onlookers.

"What are you doing now?" the Buddhist people asked.

"We are taking prayer requests and are going to ask our Heavenly Father for the things we need. This is one of the ways that we love Him with all of our soul," the Christians answered."Will you pray for us, too?" the onlookers asked.

"Sure," said one of the students, and they wrote down the prayer requests shared by the Buddhists as they shared them.

The second trainee then prayed for each prayer request and finished with a prayer of blessing. The blessing included Christians and Buddhists alike. This pleased the Buddhists because they always seek a blessing to escape their karma.

Then, the third student began to tell the story of the prodigal son. As he told the story, the onlookers listened intently and interrupted at the points of the story they did not understand. Tears filled the eyes of several onlookers when the son came back to his father and was received with no shame.

"Where did you learn this story?" the Buddhists asked.

"This story is in the holy book of the Living God," my friends shared. "We study this book, so we can love God with all of our mind. He is the living God and deserves all our love."

"This is so interesting," said the Buddhists. "We like this story and have never heard it before."

Then the third trainee asked three questions: What did this story teach us about God? About people? About how to follow Jesus?

The Buddhists listened closely, some nodding their heads in agreement, as the Powerful Worship group talked about the story. Then, it was the fourth person's turn – the practice person. He began retelling the story of the prodigal son.

"Why are you telling the story again?" asked the onlookers.

"Because the living God wants us to love Him with all our strength, and practicing the story helps us remember it. Then, we can go out and share it with others," said the Powerful Worship group.

The practice person told the story again and asked the three questions another time. More of the onlookers nodded their heads, agreeing as the Powerful Worship team talked about the story.

The Powerful Worship group decided to end their time by singing one of the songs they had sung earlier. The crowd of onlookers had continued to grow, and they smiled when they recognized the song. Several commented that it was a good song and tune.

My four friends had been sitting cross-legged on a blanket in the temple. They stood to their feet, folded the blanket, and began to leave.

Several Buddhists began to murmur among themselves. Finally, a representative approached the Powerful Worship team and said,

"We enjoyed watching you. Can you come back next week?"

The Powerful Worship group said "Yes" and walked down the mountain praising God for His many blessings and for how the Buddhists had wanted to hear more about Jesus.

The next week, not four, but eight Powerful Worship students climbed the mountain and worshiped the living God in the Buddhist temple. The crowd responded the same way as before. At the end, my friends were invited to return the next Sunday night.

This continued for several months. Each Sunday night, more people joined until there were over two hundred people practicing Powerful Worship in the Buddhist temple every week. Talk about major spiritual warfare! God continued to be praised and given glory right in the middle of a satanic stronghold! Finally, the police caught word of what was going on and came to the Buddhist temple one Sunday night. They demanded the

Christians leave and not come back. By that time, some of the Buddhists had turned to the living God and become followers of Jesus.

The actions of the police did not discourage my friends. Several Powerful Worship groups left the mountain and began to worship throughout the city. What Satan meant for evil, God turned into good.

That is one story about how believers used Powerful Worship to defeat Satan in spiritual warfare. I could tell you many more. My hope is that you will take what you have learned here and start your own Powerful Worship group. May the Lord bless your group and multiply love throughout your home, neighborhood, and city. May His glory and love spread once again throughout our land and bring the healing and hope we desperately need.

3

THE POWER OF LOVE

It is the sweet, simple things of life which are the
real ones after all.

— LAURA INGALLS WILDER

We live in a broken world that needs more love. In the previous chapters, I showed you how you can love God in a powerful, life-changing way. My prayer is you have already begun to practice some of the simple spiritual habits you are learning about in this book.

In this chapter, we are going to look at why it is important to practice these habits and the blessings they will bring to you, your family, and your friends. Love is the most powerful force in this world. It changes people. I don't know about you, but many hurts and hang-ups in my life still need to be healed and changed.

People are the same all over the world, my friend – wounded, hurting, and needing love. As missionaries in Southeast Asia, we saw people struggling through some of the most difficult trouble you can imagine. We spent time with the poorest of the poor – people struggling with poor medical care, little food, working 12 hours every day of the week, and living in makeshift housing.

Many times, we would leave a village and wonder, "How do these people make it through a day?"

Let me tell you the rest of the story, though. They had an inner happiness amid their difficulties that convicted us. When we returned to America on furloughs, people seemed so unhappy although they had so much. In fact, the more they had, the unhappier they appeared. Families in America spent more money on Friday night's pizza than families in Myanmar earned in a month. Families in Myanmar, though, were closer and cared for one another more deeply. Other mission trip teams from America have made the same observations.

We have a love shortage in America. We have all the sale items from Walmart, but what we really need is love. I have a friend who says he thinks the reason zombie movies are so popular is because many of us feel like we have become total consumers and feel dead inside. We have become zombies. If you feel like that, this chapter will give a picture of a different way to live your life.

So, let's turn to the first reason practicing the simple spiritual habits is important.

Be Fruitful and Multiply

Many folks don't feel a sense of purpose. They are going through the motions, doing what is required, but nothing touches their heart or soul on a deep level. Each day adds to the previous day and comes up short. Instead of a sense of plenty, they feel empty and abandoned. This is Satan's will, not God's.

God's first command to people was to "be fruitful and multiply". He created Eve because it was "not good for man to be alone". God wanted for men and women to marry, have children, and spread throughout the earth, caring for this world, and furthering the kingdom and reign of God. God's first command to humanity was to have physical children and enjoy a full life.

God's last command to believers was similar: "Go into all the world and make disciples." The first command was to have physical children; the last was to make disciples – spiritual children. God desired for men and women to share the gospel, make disciples, and spread the kingdom of God. Few achievements are more heartwarming than seeing someone you introduced to Jesus become a Christ-follower and grow in their faith. When they introduce others to Jesus, your joy is doubled.

Paul talks about this in 2 Timothy 2:2:

> *And entrust what you heard me say in the presence of many others as witnesses to faithful people who will be competent to teach others as well.*

We call this the "222 Principle" – 2nd Timothy 2:2. Jesus taught Paul, who taught Timothy, who would teach faithful people, who would teach others, and so on. Multiplication comes when you obey Jesus's final command to believers – go and make disciples.

Throughout the last 2,000 years, people have been making disciples who then made more disciples. At some point, someone shared Jesus with you and encouraged you to grow in your faith. If you haven't already begun, now it's your turn to do the same. Living like this halves your sorrows and doubles your joys.

I want to encourage you to live a life of multiplication and not mere addition. Some folks keep a careful tally of what they have done and how others have repaid them. They "add" or "subtract" to keep the accounts even. Living your life this way destines you to spiritual poverty and unhappiness.

Instead, be the person who multiplies their influence by being a giver in life. Let's look at a simple illustration of the difference between addition and multiplication over a lifetime.

$$2 + 2 + 2 + 2 + 2 + 2 = 12$$

$$2 \times 2 \times 2 \times 2 \times 2 \times 2 = 64$$

It doesn't take a math genius see that living a life of multiplication is the path to abundance. God never asks us to do something He doesn't also give us the grace to carry out. He commands us to be fruitful and multiply. May He give both you and I a vision for the power of multiplication in our spiritual life and the heart to share His love with everyone we know and meet.

The Sea of Galilee

God has commanded us to be fruitful and multiply. But how can you do that? I want to share one of my favorite illustrations with you. When I train people, they draw the illustration step-by-step and then practice sharing it with others. It is a great Powerful Worship lesson that casts a vision for being fruitful and multiplying your life.

Let's begin by drawing a picture like the one below. Don't worry about drawing the picture exactly to scale, for we are sharing an illustration, not a masterpiece!

There are two seas in Israel – the Dead Sea and the Sea of Galilee. So, let's label the seas.

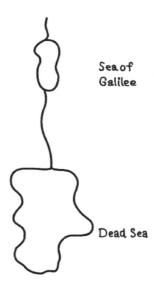

The Jordan River connects the Sea of Galilee and the Dead Sea like this:

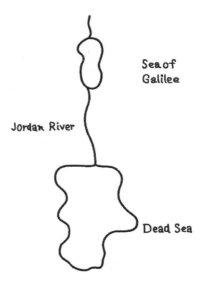

The Jordan River is an important river in the history of Israel. The Israelites crossed the Jordan river into the promised land. John the Baptist also baptized people in the Jordan River.

Now, you probably know the Sea of Galilee and the Dead Sea are different. For example, the Sea of Galilee has fish, but the Dead Sea does not. Draw fish in the Sea of Galilee and Xs in the Dead Sea.

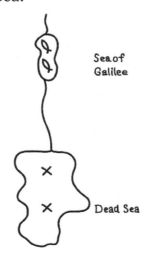

The Sea of Galilee has plants and trees surrounding it, but the Dead Sea does not. Draw trees and plants around the Sea of Galilee and Xs again by the Dead Sea.

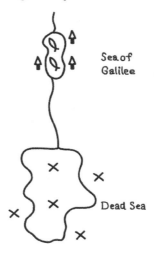

Because the Sea of Galilee has fish and trees and plants, many people live by it. No one lives by the Dead Sea because it cannot sustain life. Draw houses around the Sea of Galilee and Xs around the Dead Sea.

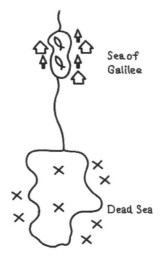

Another difference between the Sea of Galilee and the Dead Sea is famous people. Four famous people – Peter, Andrew, James, and John – lived by the Sea of Galilee. No famous people lived by the Dead Sea. Draw four stick figures and label them "Peter, Andrew, James, and John". Put four Xs beside the Dead Sea because there were no famous people living there.

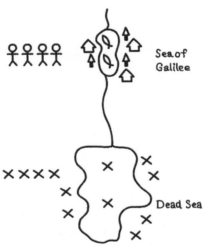

Now that the picture is complete, you can see the Sea of Galilee and the Dead Sea are as different as day and night. But the question is "Why?" Why is the Sea of Galilee teeming with life, surrounded by beautiful blooming plants and trees, and able to support whole villages while also serving as the home to famous people? Why is the Dead Sea so...well...dead? All the Dead Sea is good for is bath salts; not exactly a great claim to fame.

The difference between the Sea of Galilee and the Dead Sea is simple: The Sea of Galilee receives and gives water. The Dead Sea receives water, but does not have an outlet, so the water stagnates and cannot support life. That's why locals call it the "Dead" sea after all.

I've shared a picture of our spiritual life with you. When we receive blessings from God, we should give them to others. Then we are like the Sea of Galilee. Receiving and giving brings life to us and all those around us. If we receive and do not give, however, we are like the Dead Sea. We grow larger inside, but the water is stagnant and good for nothing. Our soul grows sick, and we bring death to ourselves and those around us.

Most people hoard the blessings of God in their lives. They don't want to share, yet they continually ask God for more and more. When their spiritual life becomes stagnant, they become unsafe people, always wanting more from God, but never satisfied. They focus on themselves. Satan fell from heaven for the same problem. He's been trying to deceive people into following his program ever since.

Jesus showed us another way. He was like the Sea of Galilee. He received love from His Father and gave love to us. He received life from His Father and gave His life for us. Jesus said it is more blessed to give than to receive. His life was like the Sea of Galilee, and He wants us to follow His example.

So which sea are you like? When God blesses you, do you bless others? Or do you keep the blessing for yourself? I want my life to be like the Sea of Galilee. My prayer is for you to want the same. I have found that you cannot out-give God financially, emotionally, physically, or any other way. Become the Sea of Galilee, and start living the full life God wants for you. It is in giving love that we discover the power of love.

Shepherds and Wolves

We've talked about several reasons to do Powerful Worship with a group. God commanded us to be fruitful and multiply – sharing Powerful Worship with others is one of the easiest and most effective ways I know to do that. Powerful Worship also enables us to be like the Sea of Galilee. We learn the simple spiritual habits, and we bless others as we have been blessed.

Now, I want to tell you a parable that will give another reason Powerful Worship is so important.

Once upon a time, a shepherd watched one hundred sheep. He loved the sheep and cared for them – leading them beside still waters and into pastures of rich green grass.

One day, though, three hungry wolves saw the flock of sheep and decided to kill one of the sheep for supper. They talked to one another and decided one wolf would distract the shepherd while the other two wolves would snatch an unsuspecting baby lamb.

Sure enough, the first wolf began to howl, and the sheep grew restless. The shepherd took his staff and headed toward the sound of the first wolf. He boldly defended his flock from the wolf and chased him off. He didn't see the other wolves sweep down from the back of the flock and steal the baby lamb.

That night, the shepherd was sad when he counted his sheep and found one was missing. He realized what had happened when he saw blood on the ground. He grew discouraged and decided he would do better the next time he heard a wolf howl.

A few days later, the wolves attacked the flock again. This time, the shepherd was ready and ran back and forth trying to keep all three wolves from his sheep. Sadly, he soon grew tired, and the wolves again took a sheep. That night, the shepherd counted ninety-eight sheep.

The shepherd tried many ways to keep the wolves from stealing his sheep: he exercised so he could run faster, and he also set up wolf traps. Unfortunately, sometimes the sheep were caught in the wolf traps, and running faster didn't help. Every few days, one more sheep disappeared from the flock.

One day, as he was watching the sheep and worrying about another wolf attack, he had an idea. Why was he trying to protect and take care of the sheep by himself? Why not ask some of his friends from the village to help defend his flock against the wolves?

So, he called his friends together, and they agreed on a plan. Each of them would guard ten sheep against the wolves. His friends hadn't been trained at Shepherd School and didn't have much experience, but they could wield a staff. The key to success wasn't their training, but willingness to work together to fight the wolves.

The next day, the wolves reappeared and were startled to see eleven shepherds instead of one, eleven staffs instead of one, and every sheep protected by a shepherd close by.

This changed everything. The wiles of the wolves no longer worked. In fact, whenever they tried to steal a sheep, one of the shepherds quickly responded and would beat them back. Now, instead of sheep getting hurt, the wolves found themselves with bruises and broken limbs.

It didn't take long for the wolves to decide that this flock wasn't worth the trouble. They moved to another valley, looking for a flock with only one shepherd.

What is the point of this parable? Simply, whenever a church expects one pastor to guard and protect the flock, Satan and his demons have no trouble attacking and harming believers in that church. When a pastor has others helping him watch over the flock, believers are protected from the Evil One and able to grow in their faith.

▼ ▼ ▼ ▼ ▼

Powerful Worship allows everyone in the church to be a part of a small group that worships, prays, studies God's Word, and practices what they have learned. Satan finds it difficult to penetrate this type of group. Powerful Worship is a mighty weapon of spiritual warfare.

May your war room be a place where believers can meet, listen to one another, obey the Great Commandment, value, and encourage one another.

We have a love shortage today. Everyone has good intentions, but we get busy and let the important things like love slip by. I have done it, and you probably have, as well.

If we want to obey the Great Commandment, we must put habits in place that will assure we obey, even when we don't realize it. Powerful Worship helps set up those simple spiritual habits.

As you have seen in this chapter, there are good reasons to practice Powerful Worship with a group of friends. Powerful Worship helps us obey God's command to multiply spiritually. Powerful Worship helps us bless others with the blessings we have received. This keeps you and I from getting stagnant in our spiritual life. Powerful Worship also protects people from the Evil One. Oh, how the shepherd heart of Jesus must weep today to see so many Christians attacked and hurt by Satan!

One of my best friends is a national in Myanmar named John.* When I met John, he had been dating Jane* (*names changed for security reasons) for fourteen years. In Myanmar, people are so poor that they wait long periods of time before they marry. They simply can't afford it or can't leave their families who depend on their salary of thirty dollars a month.

The day finally arrived when John told me he was going to marry Jane. They were excited after such a long wait and had planned a simple wedding ceremony. Our family was on furlough and unable to attend, but my parents were in Myanmar on a mission trip and stood in our place. When my parents found out that John and Jane could not afford wedding rings, they gave them beautiful gold and ruby rings as a gift. John and Jane felt richly blessed.

Several years later, I noticed that John and Jane were not wearing their wedding rings, although they were happily married and had a child. I asked John about it.

John said, "Dr. Dan, we had to sell the wedding rings. We were ministering to many people and ran out of money. Jane and I prayed about it and decided to sell the rings to keep helping others. We wanted to be like the Sea of Galilee."

John went on to tell me about the people they had ministered to and how several had given their life to Jesus and were following Him. His face beamed as he talked about the blessing it was to be a giver in life.

John and Jane had found the true joy of multiplying themselves and seeing others follow Jesus. They were like the Sea of Galilee. Because of John and Jane's ministry, believers struggling against poverty and persecution were strengthened and given hope.

While our family was overseas, people like John and Jane constantly challenged us to walk closer to Jesus. Sometimes people see missionaries as "heroes", but I want you to know the real heroes overseas are people like John and Jane. I'm also glad to report that when I shared this story in America, a church took a love offering to buy John and Jane new rings which they now proudly wear!

Be like the Sea of Galilee, and multiply love everywhere! Be a giver in life and show others what it means to be like Jesus. Let Him use you to gather a Powerful Worship group and fight the good fight in spiritual warfare.

4

LEADING POWERFUL WORSHIP

Our greatest fear should not be of failure but of
succeeding at things in life that don't really matter.

— FRANCIS CHAN

Here are the answers to some frequently asked questions that I receive about Powerful Worship.

What is a good way to start a
Powerful Worship group?

Start with your family and friends. Powerful Worship is the most meaningful when you love God with the people you love. Whether you use Powerful Worship in family devotions, prayer groups, or a discipleship group, relationships are the key.

We started having weekly family devotions with our kids using Powerful Worship. Each person would be assigned a different part and encouraged to "make it their own." As a result, all of us grew in our love for God and one another. We are a close-knit family because of Powerful Worship.

You can start a Powerful Worship group with your friends. If you are already part of a prayer group, or want to start one, Powerful Worship keeps the focus on loving God and loving people. Talking to God is always easier after worshipping Him. Your heart is open to whatever He may say. Studying scriptures on prayer and finding ways to put feet to your prayers makes Powerful Worship ideal for a prayer group.

If you and a friend have talked about deepening your faith and simplifying your spiritual life, I recommend doing Powerful Worship together. We have seen Powerful Worship groups start with two people and grow to four. As you start your group and help others to do the same, you will be blessed and surprised how easy it is to grow in your faith. Learning the simple spiritual habits in Powerful Worship produces a great harvest for the kingdom.

What are some ways people have used Powerful Worship?

Over the years, the people we have trained have used Powerful Worship in their spiritual lives in different ways. Powerful Worship is like a spiritual building block. The more you use it, the stronger your faith becomes. The fact that it is so simple allows the Holy Spirit to direct people in different ways.

I use Powerful Worship personally in my war room. I start by worshipping God, often with a worship CD or singing alone. Then, I enter a time of Bible study – learning about God's promises and power. Hearing the Word of God brings faith, so sometimes I listen to scripture on my electronic device. After my heart is tuned in to heaven and my mind is full of God's Word, I pray. If you don't have it already, I wrote a book on prayer in the war room. You can find it on Amazon. I finish my war room time with journaling and discerning what God wants me to do that day for His glory.

People have used Powerful Worship to start a prayer group. Love conquers all and practicing the simple spiritual habits in Powerful Worship equips believers to fight the good fight. Many women I know would love to pray with other women but are unsure how to start. Powerful Worship gives a simple but powerful way to obey the Great Commandment with others. Jesus promised if two or three agree on anything on earth... and Powerful Worship gives an easy way to bring people together in agreement to storm the gates of hell.

Powerful Worship groups help the pastor of a church empower others to guard and feed the body of Christ. Men and women under-shepherds protect the flock from the schemes of the evil one. Believers are given the opportunity to love one another and share life. Loneliness disappears, and love brings healing to broken hearts.

If God has called you to plant a new church, I recommend starting with Powerful Worship groups. You will be laying a good foundation and teaching people how to be doers and not hearers of the Word only. You will be leading them away from consumer-driven Christianity to obedience-based Christianity. After you have a core group, and as the Lord leads, you merely teach the group about baptism, the Lord's Supper, and giving. A group of people who are regularly practicing Powerful Worship and commit to adding the other three commands moves from being a group to becoming a church. Read through Acts 2 to see how the early church did this.

I could go on and on about ways you can be a blessing by starting a Powerful Worship group. I encourage you to be like the Sea of Galilee and give others what you have received yourself.

What does Powerful Worship look like with young children?

When our children were young, we adapted our Powerful Worship times to them. We would sing songs that had hand movements or actions they enjoyed. We would make crafts as presents to give to God in worship.

During the prayer time, we asked how we could pray for their friends. Sometimes, we put them in our laps and said a blessing prayer over them. Other times, we would give a word of testimony about how God had answered our prayers. We kept a prayer list and reminded our children about the concerns we were praying for as a family. We always included people on the mission field to cast a vision for the world to them.

The Bible study time included: simple lessons with hand motions, making a craft while talking about a Bible story, or watching a video about a Bible character. We then asked simple questions like "What would you have done in this story?" or "How do you think this character in the story felt?" Sometimes we went around the circle, each person telling a part of the story until we had completed it. We encouraged the kids to be dramatic in their retelling.

During the practice times, we practiced singing worship songs together, prayed in pairs for each other, or retold the Bible story to each other in pairs. Many times, we closed with the Lord's Prayer or by singing a song. Sometimes, the children would put on a performance for the adults showing the truths they had learned during the Powerful Worship time.

What does Powerful Worship look like with teenagers?

The main change that occurred when our kids became teenagers was that they began to lead different parts of Powerful Worship. We would assign each person in the family a part in Powerful Worship the night or morning before we worshiped. Sometimes the kids paired up to lead worship, prayer, or study. Other times, they led the section alone. We encouraged them to "make it their own". Sometimes, we chose a topic for the Powerful Worship time, but usually we depended on the Holy Spirit to speak to each person and knit the time together.

We stressed that everyone should bring something to Powerful Worship to give to the Lord. True worship is not getting but giving! Often, the kids would hear us say, "What do you have to bring to the Lord today to worship and love Him?" We worked at creating an environment where people didn't need to be perfect, but rather, sincere in their expressions of worship. Trying to be perfect is a mistake, after all.

Why do you limit the number in a Powerful Worship group to four?

We limit the number of people to four in a Powerful Worship group for several reasons. First, the purpose of Powerful Worship is to equip each person in the group to love God with all their heart, soul, mind, and strength.

Too often, Christians are spectators and not participants in worship. You will fight this temptation at every turn because it is the model you have seen in present-day churches. It is not the model Jesus shows us in the Gospels, though.

One way to keep the group at four is to meet every other week. If a fifth person comes to the group, plan their next meeting being with one of the current group members on an off-week. This will keep the first group at four and start multiplication. Then, a person is in a group where they receive and another group to which they give. Sounds like the Sea of Galilee to me!

But what should you do, if you have more people come, and they can't multiply out (for whatever reason)? I would suggest having a time of fellowship at first, singing a few worship songs together as a large group, and then splitting the large group into groups of four. Each small group then has Powerful Worship together.

End the time together by reconnecting the large group, asking for testimonies from group members about how God has worked in their heart during Powerful Worship, and ending with a worship song or prayer. This is what we do when we train large groups on how to do Powerful Worship.

We have trained up to 100 people at a time like this. When each Powerful Worship group is singing a praise song, the combination of all the groups singing is what it must sound like in heaven!

Why do you use hand motions?

I am asked often why we use hand motions in training events. People who have not been through Follow Jesus training or used hand motions before tend to see them as childish. I guess this is because we use them a lot when we teach children in American churches. I want to give you several reasons why using hand motions is important.

On the mission field, we often trained people who have received little formal education. At first, I thought this was going to be a difficult problem but later found that it forced us to take an "obedience-based" approach, rather than an "education-based" approach. We had to depend on God to lead us in how we worded our lessons and training. We also had to rely on the Holy Spirit to help each person who was receiving the training understand what we meant.

Don't get me wrong. I am a PhD and thankful for the godly scholars who have invested into my life. But all the education in the world doesn't make a difference if you don't do what Jesus said. We found that semi-illiterate people could recite everything we taught them (during a three-day training seminar) if we used hand motions. How much of the last seminar you attended can you recite from memory? Just saying...

Scientific research backs up the use of hand-motions, too. Researchers have found that people remember something six times better if it is associated with physical activity. One of the keys to developing a habit is physical association. I have found over the years that the repetitive use of hand motions has woven the simple spiritual habits into my heart, soul, mind, and body. I didn't realize it when we started, but I am thankful for it now. I want the same to happen for you.

A little common sense should be used, however. I always encourage people we train to not use the hand motions in public places, like a coffee shop or restaurant. People might gawk and wonder about your sanity. But if you are in a safe place, using the hand motions in this book will significantly increase the fruitfulness of the simple spiritual habits in your life. I have found this true especially in my war room. May God grow you into a mighty Oak of Righteousness under which the next generation can find rest and renewal.

CONCLUSION

*What you are is God's gift to you, what you become
is your gift to God.*

— HANS URS VON BALTHASAR

Why do you teach and write in a simple way? This is another question I get a lot. And I mean A LOT. It always surprises people that someone with a PhD would teach and write the way I do. You may or may not have wondered about it, but I thought I would share my heart with you just in case you have.

I'm just a simple guy who wants to love God, love people, and follow Jesus. I'm a person who has lived in this broken world long enough to be broken many times myself. Right now, I am traveling the dark valley of grief over the loss of my wife of thirty years.

I have found (and hope you have found) that abiding in Jesus is the greatest joy anyone can find this side of heaven. I want to love Him. I want to be like Him. I need Him every day in so many ways that I could fill another book talking about them. I want Him to be my all in all.

And I'm concerned about the church today. We have all the bells and whistles, but it seems to me, little of the power of God. We have every program you can imagine, but little of the transforming presence of Jesus. I'm part of the problem. You are part of the problem. All of us are part of the problem. But what is the answer?

Paul voiced a concern that the church had left the simplicity of Christ in his day. If he were writing today, I believe he would say the same and use an exclamation mark.

Living simply like Jesus is the answer, it seems to me. Jesus taught simply – so simply the uneducated could understand and, in turn, share the stories with their friends. Jesus ministered simply – His ministry didn't need fund-raising and gift books and pleas for support.

Jesus loved deeply – meeting the needs of each person where they were and not as a number to report to supporters. Jesus died simply – a man of sorrows, abandoned by his friends, and forgotten by the masses.

Jesus is the reason I teach and write the way I do. I want to be like Him. I want what I say and do to depend on the power of the Holy Spirit and not persuasive or creative words. I don't always do it well. Sometimes I fail miserably. But that is my deepest wish. I hope it is yours, too.

I've shown you a way that my family and many others have discovered to simplify our spiritual lives and grow our faith. I hope you have already tried Powerful Worship with your family or friends. My prayer is that you will develop the simple spiritual habits we have talked about in this book until they are so much a part of you that you do them without thinking.

One of my favorite parts of Follow Jesus training is the session where we show students the power of practice. Most believers are familiar with worshipping, praying, and studying the Bible in a small group. The reason Powerful Worship "works" is the practice part. Let me show you the difference practice makes.

Imagine for a moment that I am in front of 100 students at a Follow Jesus training, and you are one of the students. I tell the students I'm going to do a skit and need a volunteer. You volunteer and come to the front.

I say, "My friend and I are the same spiritually. We both worship God, pray, and study God's Word. We both share our faith, and God gives us one new believer every year. For this example, I want you to remember that my friend and I are, spiritually, on the same maturity level."

You and I show the hand motions for worship, pray, study, and practice to the students, and they copy us.

Then, I say, "We are the same spiritually, but there is one difference. My friend (you) shares about worship, prayer, and Bible study, but also has the new believers practice what they have learned. I want to show you the difference practice makes."

At this point, I have explained to the students that you and I worship, pray, and teach the Bible by using the hand motions. I have told them that God gives us one new believer each year, and so we both are going to get one person as our new believer. Both you and I go out in the crowd, select a person, and come back in front of the group with our "new believer".

I tell the students, "After one year, there is one person on my side and one person on my friend's side. We reached the same number of people. Watch my friend and their new believer, though. My friend is having their new believer practice, while I am not."

You practice the hand motions with your new believer until they do them easily. I stand by my person and talk with them, but we don't practice.

Then, I say, "Let's see what happens the second year. My new believer has only listened and not practiced, so they don't have the confidence to bring someone to Christ. So, I am the only one on my side who goes out to get a new person in year two."

I bring a new person from the audience for my side, and my group has three people standing before the students.

"My friend, however, has been practicing with his new believer, so they both have confidence to share, and God gives them both a new believer. Both go into the crowd and bring a new person back."

You and your believer get one person each and bring them up to the front.

"In year two, we start to see a difference. On my side, we have 3 people. On my friend's side, they have 4 people. I still don't practice with my people. Look at my friend's side, though. They are practicing with each another."

Each time, your side does the same thing. You and each person in your group get a "new believer" and train them using the hand motions for how to do simple worship. You are making disciples who make disciples. Every person is trained by the person who brought them to Jesus.

On my side of the room, I do everything for my new believers. I lead them in singing. I lead them in prayer. I lead them in Bible study. But everything depends on me. They never practice, so their confidence is very low.

We continue to year 3. I have 4 people after I bring my new believer up from the audience; you have 8 on your side.

In year 4, I have 5 people, and you have 16.

In year 5, I have 6 people, and you have 32.

I usually stop at this point and remind people that you and I are the same spiritually. God doesn't love you more or want to bless you more. The only difference between us is you practice with your new believer and have everyone on your side do the same. I don't.

In year 6, I add a new believer to my side and have 7 people, but your group doubles to 64 because everyone practices with their new believer and gains confidence in making disciples.

In year 7, I have 8 people, and you have 128. And we could go on and on...

When we run out of people to bring to the front, I stop the illustration and share my heart with the students.

"One day, everyone in this room is going to die and stand before Jesus. I promise the first thing you are going to do when you see Him is bow in worship. I think the second thing you will want to do is give Him something. Give Him a gift to show how much you appreciate everything He has done for you.

"When you stand before Jesus, do you want to give Him a small gift like the group of people standing with me? Or, do you want to give Him a gift like the one my friend has?"

I point to my small group of people and then to all the people in your group.

"I don't know about you, but I want to be like my friend (I point to you). I want to give Jesus a gift like this (I point to your group).

Don't forget to practice so every believer can have the confidence to obey Jesus and make disciples. Don't forget... my friend and I are the same spiritually. The only difference in how fruitful our ministries became was they practiced with their new believers."

We end the session in prayer. Students often tell me later this illustration made an incredible impact on their lives. I pray God has planted a vision of multiplication in your heart and what He can do when you are faithful in your life, too.

But you may be saying, "Dr. Dan, I am shy and don't like to be in front of people. I hear what you are saying, but don't think I could ever lead a Powerful Worship group."

I've heard that before. In fact, my wife was the first one to say that to me when we were first learning about obeying the Great Commandment by doing Powerful Worship.

Holli was shy and liked to be behind the scenes serving everyone. She embarrassed easily and didn't like being in the limelight. She loved and prayed and served. But she wasn't flashy and often wondered how God could use her like she saw others being used. It was a struggle for her. We talked about it many times.

Jesus described himself as gentle and lowly of spirit, but it seems like one must be assertive and loud to be successful in today's Christian culture. Jesus often withdrew from the crowd and didn't seek fame or fortune. So much of what goes on today is not like that at all. Holli loved Jesus and served Him in simple ways in a world dead-set on big buildings, big budgets, and big numbers.

Despite her hesitation, she began to mentor small groups of students and women. She taught them Powerful Worship, and they taught their friends. They worshiped together. They prayed for their kids and husbands and church together. They opened God's Word and asked the Spirit of God to teach them how to obey from a heart of love. Simple. Spiritual. Life-giving. That was my wife. And she was shy.

In October 2015, we learned she had ovarian cancer. We prayed. We cried. We sought the Lord's face for healing. But God took her home in March 2016. She closed her eyes on this side of the river and opened them to see the face of the Savior she loved so much. The kids and I miss her more than I can tell you.

What happened next is why I am sharing this story with you.

Hundreds of notes and letters from across the world began to pour into our mailbox. Message after message on Facebook shared the same thoughts. Many women testified to the difference Holli had made in their lives.

They shared how the simple, practical truths she had taught them and who she was had made an enduring impact in their lives. By the grace of God, a woman who wondered how she could ever make a difference had created a huge gift for Jesus in her ministry. Well done, precious wife, well done!

That brings it back to me and you and all you've learned in this little book. It isn't an accident that you found this book. God has been moving in your heart, giving you the desire to read all the way to the end. What is He saying to you? What will you do now?

My prayer is that you gather your family or friends and begin to love God with all your heart, soul, mind, and strength. It won't be flashy. But it will be real. And God will change you little by little.

As you love Him, He will heal you and strengthen you with His love. You will be a safe place where others can find healing, too. You will be like the Sea of Galilee – receiving blessings from God and giving them to others. You can do this, my friend. God is with you.

THANK YOU

BEFORE YOU GO, I'd like to say "thank you" again for buying this guide to start a powerful group that worships, prays, studies God's word, and practices what they have learned. I know you could have picked from dozens of books, but you chose this one. My prayer is this book has been a blessing to your life.

Now I'd like to ask for a *small* favor. Could you please take a minute or two and leave a short review for this book at go.lightkeeperbooks.com/e-pww-rev? There is no greater way to thank me than this!

Think of it as a testimony to other believers about how this book helped you and could benefit them. You can help me help others.

And if you loved it, then please let me know that too!

BONUS

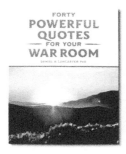  

Don't forget to download your free *Powerful Prayers Bonus Pak*! The free *Powerful Prayers Bonus Pak* includes three resources to help you pray powerful prayers:

- 100 Promises – Audio Version
- 40 Faith-Building Quotes
- 40 Powerful Prayers.

All are suitable for framing. To download your free Powerful Prayers Bonus Pak, visit: go.lightkeeperbooks.com/powerpak

I've also included an excerpt from my bestselling book *Powerful Jesus in the War Room*. God has blessed many through this book and I wanted to give you a chance to "try before you buy." To order *Powerful Jesus in the War Room*, go to go.lightkeeperbooks.com/e-pjw.

If you liked *Powerful Worship in the War Room,* please leave a review. Your feedback will help other believers find this book easier and encourage me in my calling to write practical, powerful books to encourage, equip, and empower Christians throughout the world.

POWERFUL
JESUS
—— ## IN THE ——
WAR ROOM

DANIEL B LANCASTER PhD

INTRODUCTION

Grant Lord, that I may know myself that I may know Thee.

– AUGUSTINE OF HIPPO

In this broken world, it is hard for people to accept themselves. Because people don't accept themselves, it is hard to love others too—with a deep love that transforms people, the love others need to feel.

If you are like me, you want acceptance and love to permeate your life, but it is hard to come by. Just saying. A friend of mine told me "hurting people hurt people" and I've found that to be so true in my life. The problem is... all of us are hurting people.

Almost twenty years ago, my wife and I started on a journey of spiritual growth based on eight pictures of Jesus. A picture is worth a thousand words and we discovered that God had given us pictures in the Bible to help us become more like Jesus. Sounds simple and it can be. I'm going to show you how to grow in Christ.

In the process, you will discover how to really accept yourself and love others like you never thought possible. If you have read my previous books, you know I don't share theories—just practical action plans that have worked in my life and the lives of many others.

I'm excited you chose this book because I know it is going to change your life. The lessons I am going to share with you have been life-changing for my family, my co-workers, many others, and me. The solutions were developed while our family started two churches in America and refined further as we trained 5,000 nationals in Southeast Asia as missionaries. I've seen people's lives changed repeatedly. I look forward to hearing from you when God does the same in your life.

So, in this book I'm going to share the eight main pictures of Jesus in the Bible. Jesus fulfilled each of these eight pictures completely and perfectly. God has made people in such a way that they are usually strong in two of the pictures but need other pictures to complete them.

This book will teach you why people experience conflict and how you can bring people into unity as a peacemaker. It will look at each of the pictures through the lens of living in the Spirit, from a neutral point of view, or living in the flesh. I will show you a path of spiritual growth that the Lord takes people through as they become more Christlike. When you understand this path, the journey becomes more automatic and less stressful.

My wife and I used these eight pictures of Jesus in our parenting. Raising three boys and one girl is no small task. When we had our first son, it was easy because it was double coverage (to use a football defense analogy). We moved to man-on-man coverage with the birth of our second son. With the birth of our precious daughter, we had to go to zone defense. I remember when our fourth child, a son, came into the world. We moved to prevent defense. Just don't let them score, baby, don't let them score.

Seriously, the eight pictures of Jesus allowed us to raise passionate, spiritual leaders and bring healing to the nations. We cooperated with what God was doing, rather than trying to figure out our own plans. Each child had strengths in a different picture of Jesus. The tool I'm going to share with you allowed my wife and me to raise a family filled with faith, hope, and love. By God's grace, each of our children has continued as a passionate, spiritual leader to bring healing to the nations.

No one is perfect, but God is good; becoming more like Jesus is a gift he gives those who follow him. After reading this book, you will have the tools you will need to accept yourself, love others, resolve conflicts, and help your family, co-workers, church family, or community experience the healing power of God's love.

In the next chapter, I'm going to show you how to accept yourself. Before you turn the page, however, let me pray.

Lord Jesus,

Thank you for my friend. Thank you for bringing us together in a conversation that changed my life and will change theirs as they read this book.

In your wisdom, you have connected us and will bless as we journey through this book together.

Lord, I'm going to learn even more about you as I write and I thank you for that. You are so good.

You love us and transform our brokenness.

Thank you.

Lord, my friend is going to learn more about you and a simple way to grow in self-acceptance and love. You know I have struggled with my self-image and how difficult it makes living life sometimes.

Set my readers free, precious Jesus, like you set me free. Fill them with faith, hope,

and love for this journey.

May they feel you holding them so very, very close.

Please anoint my words, holy Jesus. This book means little if my friend doesn't fall more

in love with you as they read.

In your name. Amen

1

WHO AM I?

God loves you just the way you are, but He refuses to
leave you that way. He wants you to be just like Jesus.

— MAX LUCADO

The biggest barrier to accepting yourself is not understanding how God has made you. When you don't understand the masterpiece, He is making in you, you may get down on yourself and wish you were like "so-and-so." Comparing yourself with others will always lead to not accepting yourself.

In this section, I'm going to show you how to identify which of the eight main personality types God has designed you to be. God made you a certain way and wants you to discover your purpose. Understanding your personality type will give you a deep self-acceptance not affected by circumstances.

My parents divorced when I was fifteen and it wasn't pretty. As a result, I struggled for years with my self-image and self-acceptance. It wasn't until God showed me how he had made me and how much he accepted and loved me that I began to heal. If you find yourself at a similar place, I pray God will use the truths in this book to heal you, too.

As you work through the following exercise, pay attention to what God is speaking deep in your soul. Open your heart to the Holy Spirit. You can discover which of the eight personality types you are in fewer than three minutes and it doesn't cost a dime. What you learn, however, will begin transforming you from the inside out.

So, let's start on the journey. Let me help you find the real you. By the way, doing this exercise with friends and family will make for a very entertaining evening!

Finding Yourself

Start by taking a blank sheet of paper and a pencil. That's all you will need to discover your personality type.

Draw a big circle in the middle of the sheet of paper. The circle represents the whole world and every person living on it. You can find the eight personalities throughout the world in every country and culture.

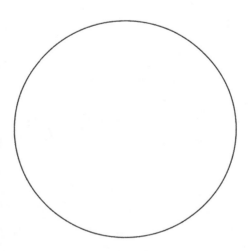

Next, draw a line from left to right and cut the circle in half. On the left side of the circle write the word "task" and on the right side of the circle write the word "people." Draw a short, vertical line to cut the line in half like the picture below.

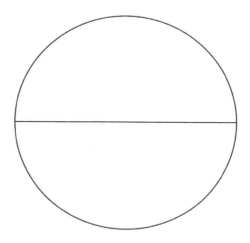

The world has two basic types of people: task-oriented and people-oriented. The horizontal line represents all those people. Task-oriented people say, "Let's get the work done and then we will play." People-oriented people say, "Let's figure out a way to make this work fun."

Put a dot on the line at the place that best represents the person you are. Before you choose, though, let me make a few comments about this line. First, after God created humanity, He said, "It is good." Wherever you placed yourself on the line—more task-oriented or relationship-oriented—is good. God has created you in a certain way for his glory.

Second, every person has "task" and "people" qualities within them. The line shows which one you stress more. If you are on the "task" side, it doesn't mean you don't care about people, and the other way around. People can care a great deal for others and be task-oriented. People-oriented people can still get the job done.

The last direction I'll give is you can't choose the middle. Sorry. I know you may be half-and-half, but please pick one side or the other. I feel your pain because I have the same trouble.

Okay. It's time to decide where you are on the circle. I have drawn a dot on the task/people line as an example of how a person slightly more task-oriented would choose.

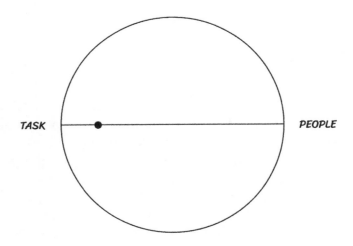

Now, draw a line from the top of the circle to the bottom, making four parts. Label the top of the circle as "extrovert" and the bottom "introvert."

Every person in the world also falls into one of two additional groups: outward-oriented or inward-oriented. Neither group is better than the other one. This is just the way God made people.

Extroverts know many people a little and draw energy from relating with other people. Introverts know a few people well and derive their energy from being alone. If you "never met a stranger," you are an extrovert. If you "think carefully before you speak," you are an introvert.

Choose a point on the extrovert/introvert line that best represents the real you. If you are very outgoing, pick near the top of the circle. If you are really private, choose near the bottom of the circle. Again, you can't select the middle. You'll see why in a second.

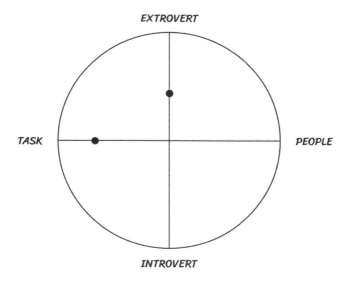

The next step is to discover where on the circle your two marks intersect. Look at the diagram on the next page to see what I'm describing as I give you the instructions.

Draw a dotted line from the dot you drew on the task/people parallel to the extrovert/introvert line until you are right across from your extrovert/introvert dot.

Then, draw a dotted line across from the extrovert/introvert line until you meet the first dotted line you created. Put a star where they come together. This star will help you discover which of the eight personality types you are in a few moments.

The final step before we talk about the eight personality types is to draw two diagonal lines (an "X") across the circle.

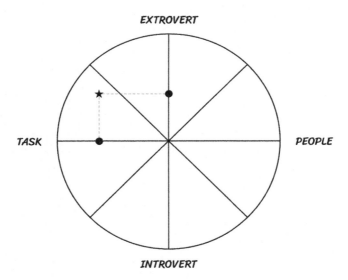

Your circle should now have eight equal pieces and look a little bit like a pizza. Here is a diagram to help you complete this step:

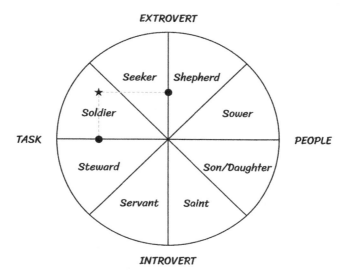

Congratulations! You now have a simple diagram that represents the world with eight different personality types. Now, let's look at short descriptions of each personality type. I'll give you a thumbnail sketch of each one so you can compare the diagram with your own experience. Feel free to read the description of the personality type where your star falls. Then, read the descriptions of the different personality types of people in your life.

You can purchase *Powerful Jesus in the War Room* at go.lightkeeperbooks.com/e-pjw.

MORE FROM THIS AUTHOR

#1 Best Sellers

on

amazon

This series on powerful prayer, heart-felt worship, and intimacy with Christ will help strengthen your "War Room" and give you a battle plan for prayer.

Visit go.lightkeeperbooks.com/battleplan to learn more.

CHRISTIAN SELF-HELP

Available on

amazon

Overcome fear, shame, and other spiritual attacks
that hold you back from being all God created you to be.

Visit go.lightkeeperbooks.com/selfhelp to learn more

Lightkeeper Kids Series

ABOUT THE AUTHOR

Daniel B Lancaster (PhD) enjoys training others to become passionate followers of Christ. He has planted two churches in America and trained over 5,000 people in Southeast Asia as a strategy coordinator with the International Mission  Board. He served as Assistant Vice-President for University Ministries at Union University and currently is a international missionary with Cornerstone International. He has four grown children and a delightful grandson.

Dr. Dan is available for speaking and training events. Contact him at dan@lightkeeperbooks.com to arrange a meeting for your group.

Made in the USA
Monee, IL
17 April 2023

31998844R00059